Trouble
in the
ROCKIES

Adam Guillain
Illustrated by Stephen Elford

Dorset County Library	
Askews	2009
	£5.25

Dorset Libraries
Withdrawn Stock

D0242978

Chapter 1 – The dream holiday

Tom Li logged on to his blog on the family website.

"This year's holiday is going to be the best ever!" Dad said.

"A real dream holiday," agreed Mum, "to a very special place."

April 10

Posted by Tom

Time to plan this year's holiday! We started by looking at photos from some of our other holidays. As you can see, we love cycling!

THE LONDON EYE, ENGLAND

LOCH NESS, SCOTLAND

THE EIFFEL TOWER, FRANCE

The Li family had been saving up for a trip to the Rockies in Canada.

"Will we see wild animals?" Amy asked.

"I hope so," said Tom. He showed them a website that he'd found.

"Look, there are cougars, too!" he said.

"She's beautiful," Amy sighed when she saw the cougar.

"She is," said Mum, "but I wouldn't like to meet her in the wild!"

Banff National Park Canada

Cougars

Habitat	Mountains and jungle
Colouring	Brown with light patches
Hunts	Anything it can catch
Speed	72 kph
Status	Under threat

It was Dad who found the cycle route through a dramatic valley.

"That looks amazing!" Amy and Tom agreed.

"And safe enough," Dad said, "as long as we hire a local guide."

With the click of a button, he booked the family trip to Banff National Park in the Rockies.

"You can write all about it on your blog, Tom," Mum grinned.

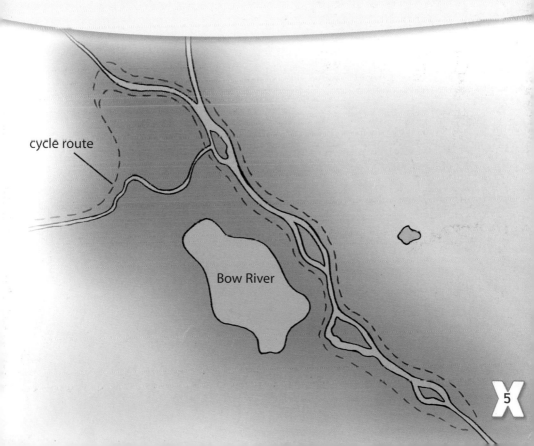

cycle route

Bow River

And that's exactly what Tom did.

Day 1

Posted by Tom

We had dinner AND breakfast on the plane! Amy and I watched a film about all the things we could do in the National Park. But it was a long flight – and THEN we had to take a bus to the campsite in Banff!

BANFF NATIONAL PARK

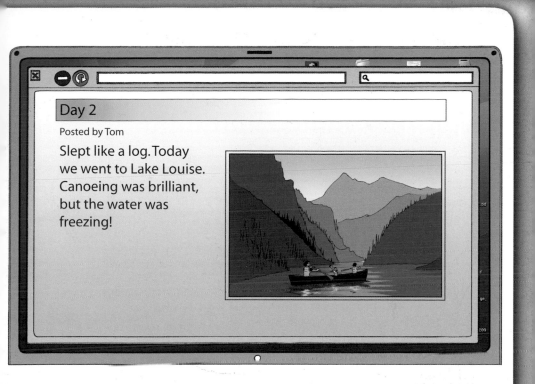

Day 2

Posted by Tom

Slept like a log. Today we went to Lake Louise. Canoeing was brilliant, but the water was freezing!

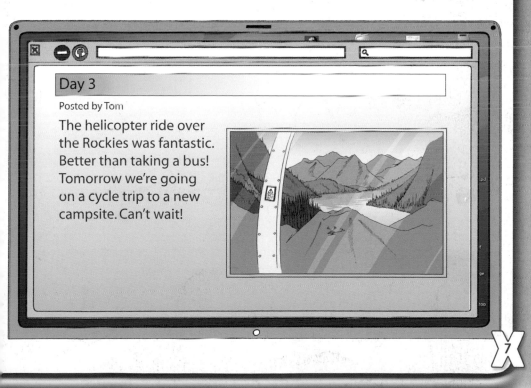

Day 3

Posted by Tom

The helicopter ride over the Rockies was fantastic. Better than taking a bus! Tomorrow we're going on a cycle trip to a new campsite. Can't wait!

Chapter 2 – Disaster strikes

Day four started as planned. Dad hired bikes and a guide.

"This is Eric, our guide," said Dad. "He knows the Rockies really well."

"The ride to your next campsite is beautiful," Eric told them. "If we're lucky, we might see some bears."

"Wow!" said Amy.

"I told you we would see wild animals," said Tom.

"Will we be safe?" asked Mum.

"Yes," said Eric, "as long as you all stay with me."

EMERGENCY SUPPLIES

The family was excited as Eric led them down a long, winding path.

"Stay in first gear and use your brakes," he told them. "We will soon be on the valley trail."

The trail was quite flat and the view was
breath-taking. They cycled all morning and
had a picnic lunch on a rock looking out over
the valley.

"Will we see any cougars?" Tom asked Eric.

"I'm not hopeful, Tom. Cougars are becoming endangered, even here," said Eric sadly. "The best time to see them is at dusk when they come out to hunt."

"And by then, we will be at the campsite," said Dad.

"Remember, this is where these animals live," Eric continued. "We must try not to frighten them."

After lunch they set off again. By late afternoon the Ryans were getting tired.

"Are we nearly there ... " started Amy. But before she could finish, something up ahead made her gasp with excitement.

"I think I can see something too ... shhh," Eric hushed. "There are bears in the valley!"

They all stopped and quickly got off their bikes.

"Follow me," said Eric quietly. "We'll find a safe place to watch them."

"They're fishing," Eric whispered.

"They look so big, even from here," said Tom.

Mum smiled. "This is close enough for me."

Suddenly there was a loud noise. Dad looked around with alarm. "What was that?" he asked.

A sudden landslide of rocks and stones swept Tom and his mum off their feet.

"Aaah!" they cried as they tumbled and slid down towards the river.

Chapter 3 – No escape

Tom and Mum fell down the bumpy slope, through some prickly bushes then – splash!

Tom was shocked by the cold water.

"Mum!" he gasped. His heart was racing with fear. "Mum, where are you?"

"Tom!"

Tom saw his mum's head bobbing up and down in the water. He swam across to her.

"Swim to the bank," she shouted. But the strong currents made it impossible.

As the currents got faster and faster, Tom and his mum began to spin. Tom felt his helmet crash against a rock. "This is it," he shivered.

Mum held onto a rock and grabbed Tom's hand. Just then, he spotted two bears on the riverbank.

"Watch out!" he cried.

Mum quickly let go of the rock.

"Keep hold of my hand!" she shouted to Tom.

Tom clutched his mum's hand tightly.

The currents got faster and faster, taking them away from the bears. Tom was terrified that they were never going to stop.

Eventually they slowed down and the river became much calmer. Relieved, Tom felt his feet touch the bottom of the river. He stood up and helped his mum to the bank.

"There must have been a landslide," Mum panted. "I'm glad we had our helmets on."

In the fading light, Tom thought he saw something slither through the long grass.

"Snakes!" he gasped.

They stared into the grass, but nothing moved. Tom thought his mind must have been playing tricks on him.

"What do you think happened to the others?" asked Tom.

"I saw them on the slope," said Mum. "The bushes must have broken their fall."

"Dad and Amy have phones. I hope they can get a signal and call for help," Tom said.

"And Eric has flares," said Mum. "I saw one go off. Don't worry, Tom. Someone will come and rescue us soon."

Tom saw that his mum was in pain.

"What's wrong?" he asked.

"I've hurt my ankle, that's all," she said.

Then there was a noise in the bushes.

They looked around and in the distance

they saw... a cougar!

Meanwhile...

Amy, Dad and Eric picked themselves up
and looked around. "Where's Mum? Where's
Tom?" Dad shouted.

"They're in the river!" Amy cried.

Dad wanted to go straight after them.

"No!" said Eric. "The current is too fast."

Amy and Dad knew that Tom and Mum were good swimmers, but they were still worried. Eric grabbed a red flare from his bag and set it off. Dad tried his phone.

"You won't get a signal here," said Eric. "We must follow them on our bikes. I'll come back for their bikes later."

Chapter 4 – In for the kill

It was nearly dark now and the cougar was getting closer. Tom and Mum were scared. Slowly, quietly, they started to walk away.

"The others will soon be here to help us," said Mum comfortingly.

"I know," said Tom, trying to sound brave.

But Tom's heart was beating fast. "The cougar is moving in for the kill," he thought. He could hear her approaching. Suddenly, a loud noise made them gasp. A red flare shot into the sky and the cougar leapt away.

"It's Eric!" cried Tom.

Tom and Mum looked up to see Eric leading Dad and Amy down the slope.

"It's OK," shouted Eric. "She wouldn't hurt you. She just wanted a closer look at you."

Dad ran towards Tom and Mum to check they were alright. Amy followed closely behind him.

Soon the Li family were all together again.

"I'm sorry it took us so long to find you," said Eric. "The cycle route was covered with rocks after the landslide. We had to carry the bikes part of the way."

Eric checked Mum's ankle. "We'll need to get that x-rayed," he said.

Then a strange sound filled the sky.

"It's a helicopter," Amy cried.

Everyone looked up.

"It's the rescue team," shouted Eric. "They saw the flare!"

Everyone cheered.

"I hope you're going to write up this amazing adventure on your blog," Mum smiled to Tom.

April 10

Posted by Tom

The rescue team took us all back to the campsite in Banff. The view from the helicopter was awesome. Even with Mum's injury, there was loads we could do – bird-watching, horse riding and more canoeing.

It's funny. We planned this holiday to be the best one ever. But we never planned for our bike ride to be the journey of a lifetime!

>> DAY 4